HEALING A TEEN'S
GRIEVING HEART

Also by Alan Wolfelt:

Creating Meaningful Funeral Ceremonies:
A Guide for Families

Healing a Child's Grieving Heart:
100 Practical Ideas for Families,
Friends and Caregivers

Healing Your Grieving Heart
for Teens: 100 Practical Ideas

Healing a Friend's Grieving Heart:
100 Practical Ideas for Helping Someone
You Love Through Loss

Healing Your Grieving Heart for Kids:
100 Practical Ideas

The Journey Through Grief:
Reflections on Healing

Understanding Your Grief:
Ten Essential Touchstones for Finding
Hope and Healing Your Heart

The Wilderness of Grief: Finding Your Way

Companion Press is dedicated to the education and support of both the bereaved and bereavement caregivers. We believe that those who companion the bereaved by walking with them as they journey in grief have a wondrous opportunity: to help others embrace and grow through grief—and to lead fuller, more deeply-lived lives themselves because of this important ministry.

Companion
P R E S S

For a complete catalog and ordering information, write or call:

Companion Press
The Center for Loss and Life Transition
3735 Broken Bow Road
Fort Collins, CO 80526
(970) 226-6050
www.centerforloss.com

HEALING A TEEN'S GRIEVING HEART

100 PRACTICAL IDEAS FOR FAMILIES, FRIENDS & CAREGIVERS

ALAN D. WOLFELT, PH.D.

Companion
PRESS

Fort Collins, Colorado
An imprint of the Center for Loss and Life Transition

Companion Press is an imprint of the
Center for Loss and Life Transition,
3735 Broken Bow Road, Fort Collins, Colorado 80526
970-226-6050
www.centerforloss.com

Companion Press books may be purchased in bulk for
sales promotions, premiums or fundraisers. Please
contact the publisher at the above address for more
information.

Printed in the United States of America

12 11 10 09   5 4 3 2

ISBN: 978-1-879651-24-1

To my precious daughter, Megan. Thanks for inspiring me to write a book that will help teens mourn well so they can live well and love well.

Introduction

"Before I can walk in another's shoes
I must first remove my own."
—Author unknown

We tend to think of adolescence as a time for fun and rebellion and growing independence—not a time for profound loss. Yet each year millions of teenagers suffer the death of a parent, a grandparent, a sibling, a teacher, a friend. The recent school shootings, particularly the Columbine tragedy (which took place just an hour from where I live), have made us more acutely aware of this painful demographic.

As a grief counselor and Director of the Center for Loss and Life Transition (and parent to three children, one an amazing daughter on the cusp of adolescence), I've had the honor of working with hundreds of grieving teenagers. They have taught me that, because of their already challenging life phase, their experience with grief is unique. They are not children, yet neither are they adults. Instead, teens comprise a special group of mourners who deserve a special kind of care and consideration from the adults around them. Grieving teens need our help if they are to survive what to them often seem unsurvivable.

I like to say that grieving teens need us to be a "companion" to them as they journey through grief. To "companion" grieving teenagers means to be present to them and attentive to their needs and communication. It means allowing them to teach us what their unique grief journeys are like instead of us telling them what they should or should not do. It means, as the quote above points out, removing our shoes before we walk in theirs. It means honoring and bearing witness to their pain without trying to take the pain away or protecting them from the truth. It means making the commitment to be there for them, now and in the months and years ahead.

I'd also like to point out the important distinction between the terms *grief* and *mourning*. Grief is the internal thoughts and feelings of loss and pain when someone loved dies, whereas mourning is the outward, shared expression of that grief—or grief gone public. All teens grieve when someone they love dies. But if they are to heal, they must have a safe, accepting atmosphere in which they can mourn.

Now let's look at some of the typical aspects of teen grief. Keep in mind that these are merely general guidelines; don't expect every grieving teen to conform to the precepts that follow. Instead, read this introduction for background knowledge then put it aside as you concentrate on letting each grieving teen teach you what her unique grief journey is like for her.

Developmental Tasks Complicated By Grief

With the exception of infancy, no developmental period is so filled with change as adolescence. One of the primary changes teenagers must go through is separating from their families. Leaving the security of childhood, teenagers begin to separate from their parents and siblings and establish their own identities. This process is normal and necessary (although trying!); without it, teens would never be able to leave home, establish careers or have families of their own.

But as many of us know from our experiences, separating isn't always easy. With the need to separate often comes the need to devalue those closest to us. Fights with parents and siblings are common. So, when a parent or sibling whom the teen has been at odds with dies, the teen may feel a sense of regret or unfinished business.

In addition, even though teens need to separate from their families, they still want to feel loved and secure. This ambivalence can naturally complicate the grief journey. The teen may unconsciously think, "If I mourn, that means I need you. But my stronger need right now is for autonomy, so I don't want to mourn."

As teenagers separate from their families, they attach more to their peer group. Friends, including boyfriends and girlfriends, may become the teen's most important source of affirmation and acceptance. So, if a teen's friend should die, the hurt can be particularly painful. Also remember that for a teen, the death of a friend or sibling is the death of another young person. Not only will the teen probably feel despair and outrage at this injustice, but the death can also make the teen aware, perhaps for the first time, that he or she will die, too.

Because adolescence is often accompanied by awkward physical development, many teenagers feel unattractive. This can compromise their self-esteem and make them feel that much more overwhelmed by their grief. The teenager's changing outward appearance can also make them look like men and women. Too often adults take this to mean that grieving teens are emotionally mature and can "handle" their own grief. Not so. No one, especially a young person, should have to cope with their grief alone. Grieving teenagers need the love and support of adults if they are to become emotionally healthy adults themselves.

School and sometimes jobs are also a normal and necessary part of the teenager's world. In fact, both help them discover who they are and move toward independence. The death of someone loved, however, can put school and jobs on hold for a time. This, too, is normal. Grieving teens should not be expected to continue on with school and work as if nothing has happened, yet in our culture they often are. Actually, the work of mourning must take precedence if a teen is to heal. Parents, teachers and other concerned adults should understand and even encourage this temporary shift in priorities.

We've said adolescence is naturally stressful because of the developmental tasks teens must undertake. For the bereaved teen, this combination of normal challenges and the experience of grief can potentially be overwhelming. Don't be surprised if seemingly minor stresses make the bereaved teen very upset. The grieving teen might cry or get angry because her locker is stuck or she misplaced a book. Many teens need help to understand that this reaction is normal.

One last point here is that teens often do "catch-up" mourning at developmental milestones. Important events like prom or high school graduation may cause the grieving teen to feel particularly sad because the person who died isn't there to share the moment. This occurrence is normal not only shortly after the death, but also years later. In fact, many grieving teens will continue to do catch-up mourning as they enter adulthood and reach other milestones like marrying or having children.

Nature Of Deaths

Let's talk for a moment about the nature of the deaths a teenager is likely to encounter.

For many teens, the first special person in their life to die is a grandparent. If the teen was close to Grandma or Grandpa, this death can be a very significant loss and should be recognized as such. Too often the teen will hear others say "She was very old and sick anyway" or "He lived a long, full life." The fact that the grandparent was old does not take away the teen's right to mourn.

The death of a pet can also be very painful for adolescents. Sometimes they have grown up with the pet and have spent years caring for, playing and sleeping with it. Teens who have emotionally distanced themselves from family members may actually be more bonded to the pet than they are to people. As a caring adult, you can validate the teen's need to mourn this loss. You can also use the experience as an opportunity to talk about death and grief in general.

Most of the other deaths that teens experience are sudden or untimely. A parent may die of a heart attack, a brother or sister may die of cancer, or a friend may complete suicide or be killed in a car accident. The very nature of these deaths often causes the teen to feel a prolonged and heightened sense of unreality.

Of course, the death of a parent is especially difficult for young people. Teenagers expect their parents to grow old and be grandparents to the children they may eventually have. A parent's premature death, then, is the death of not only the teen's present family life but also his dreams for the future.

Similarly, the death of a brother or sister is extremely painful. The teen not only has to cope with his own grief but bear witness to the very intense grief of his parents and family. This can be an overwhelming situation—and one in which the teen's parents, understandably, are often too preoccupied to help the teen. The support of other caring adults is particularly important in such instances.

As we have already said, teens can also be extremely close to boyfriends, girlfriends and best friends. If one of these important people should die, teens need the opportunity to mourn. Unfortunately, their grief is not always acknowledged because society tends to focus on the "primary" mourners: the dead young person's immediate family. You can help by making sure the teen is included in the funeral and supported as a "primary" mourner.

The young person's heightened emotions often take the form of rage after a sudden death. Anger is a way for the teen to say, "I protest this death" and to vent her feelings of helplessness. Rage fantasies are also common. For example, if a teen's mom was killed in a car crash, the teen may express a desire to murder the drunk driver at fault. Try not to be frightened by this rage. It is a normal grief response, and most teens know not to act upon these feelings. However, some will need help in exploring the distinction between feeling rage and taking action.

If someone loved dies after a long illness, keep in mind that the teen probably began the grief process long before the actual death.

However, the teen's need to push away painful realities is stronger than an adult's, so teens sometimes feel a greater sense of shock and numbness when the person who has been ill dies. Young people who have had accurate information about the terminal illness withheld from them are also likely to feel shocked when the person dies. Finally, understand that after the extended illness of someone they love, teens may feel a sense of relief. This, too, is normal and in no way equals a lack of love for the person who died.

The Grieving Teen's Support Systems

Another critical influence on a teen's grief is their support systems. Many people assume that the grieving adolescent's friends and family members will support them in their grief journeys. In reality, this may not be true at all.

It's also not unusual that the teen's surviving parent or siblings may not be able to offer support because they are so overwhelmed by their own grief. This is natural and shouldn't be considered selfish or wrong, but it does mean that the teen will need extra support and caring from non-family members during this difficult time.

The grieving teen's lack of support may also relate to social expectations. Teens are usually expected to be "grown up" and support other members of the family, particularly a surviving parent or younger brothers and sisters. Many teens have been told, "Now you will have to take care of your family." The problem is this: When a teenager feels responsible for "taking care of the family," he or she doesn't have the opportunity, or the permission, to mourn.

Sometimes we assume that teenagers will find comfort from their peers. When it comes to death, this may or may not be true. Many grieving teens are actually greeted with indifference by their peers. It seems that unless their friends have experienced grief themselves, they project their feelings of helplessness by ignoring the subject of loss entirely. Worse yet, some of the teenager's peers may be insensitive or even cruel. It's not unusual to see peers avoid the grieving teen out of an unconscious fear that death might become a part of their lives, as well. Or, sometimes peers try to force the grieving teen to avoid the pain of grief and just get on with life. I call this "buck-up therapy." Some teens seem to be more comfortable sharing the good times than the bad. You can help by teaching teens what being a good friend in grief means.

Living With Grief

This book was written to help you be a good friend—a companion—to teens in grief. As promised, it contains 100 practical ideas for helping grieving teenagers. Some of the ideas teach the general principles of grief and mourning; the remainder offer practical do's and don'ts and suggestions for activities you can do with or for the grieving teen.

Remember that the death of someone loved is a shattering experience for young people. As a result of this death, the teen's life is under reconstruction. Consider the significance of the loss and be gentle and compassionate in all your helping efforts. Remember, too, that teens never "get over" their grief. No one gets over grief. Instead, we learn to live with it.

With support and understanding, grieving teens usually learn early on that humans do not have complete control over themselves and their world. They learn that grief is the natural counterpoint to having loved. They learn that faith and hope are central to finding meaning in whatever one does in this short life. And they learn a true appreciation for the joys of living.

Thank you for joining me in my efforts to make a difference in the lives of grieving teenagers. I salute you and I wish you all the best.

Alan D. Wolfelt

1.

Understand the difference between grief and mourning.

- Grief is the constellation of internal thoughts and feelings we have when someone loved dies. Mourning is the outward expression of our grief.

- All teens grieve when someone loved dies. But if they are to reconcile the loss, they must have a safe, accepting atmosphere in which they can mourn.

- Often teenagers don't want to mourn because mourning makes them feel vulnerable and dependent. And feeling vulnerable and dependent runs counter to their natural need to separate from parents and other authority figures.

- Grieving teens need permission to mourn. Sometimes what they need most from adults is an awareness that it is OK to feel the many emotions they feel and to talk or not talk about those emotions.

Carpe diem

When you were a teenager, did someone you love die? If so, did you mourn the death or did you just grieve, bottling up your feelings inside?

2.

Make a "contact pact" with yourself.

- Commit to contacting the teen once a week or once a month.

- Vary your means and time of contact so the teen won't feel she's just an item on your "to do" list.

- Your contact needn't take a lot of time; a brief phone call or a short note are enough to demonstrate your support. Many teens appreciate doing instead of talking. Take her to a movie or out for pizza.

- Don't neglect the teen as time passes; mourners of all ages need support long after the event of the death.

Carpe diem

Get our your daily planner right now and pencil in days on which you will, without fail, get in touch with the teen. Plan out an entire year.

3.

UNDERSTAND THE SIX NEEDS OF MOURNING

Need 1. Acknowledge the reality of the death.

- To move toward reconciliation, teenagers must, over time and with the gentle understanding of those around them, openly acknowledge that someone they love has died and will not return.

- Don't expect young people to acknowledge the reality and finality of the death in the same way adults do. Some teens, especially younger ones, will embrace the reality slowly and may even seem indifferent at times. A full sense of loss does not typically come about until several months after the death and may not occur until much later.

- As you talk with and listen to the teen, be honest about the nature and cause of the death—even if the death was violent or self-inflicted. Teens can cope with what they know; they cannot cope with what they don't know.

Carpe diem

Today, talk about the physical reality of the death. Don't assume that just because he's a teenager he really understands from a medical standpoint what cancer or a heart attack or an aneurysm is. Make sure he understands how and why the person died.

4.

UNDERSTAND THE SIX NEEDS OF MOURNING

Need 2. Move toward the pain of the loss.

- Another important need for teens is to embrace the pain of the loss. This need involves encouraging the young person to embrace all the thoughts and feelings that result from the death.

- Like the need to acknowledge the reality of the death, this need is often quashed by adults who want to protect young people from pain. Yet, as Helen Keller said years ago, "The only way to get to the other side is to go through the door."

- Keep in mind that the teen's naturally strong resistance to mourning does not mean the teen isn't hurting inside or isn't capable of mourning with support and understanding.

- Also remember that because teens don't articulate their feelings well, they often do as much if not more of their mourning through behaviors rather than words.

Carpe diem

Do something physical with the teen—shoot hoops or go for a hike or rollerblade. After the two of you had have some "warm up" time together, ask him how he's feeling about the death.

5.

UNDERSTAND THE SIX NEEDS OF MOURNING

Need 3. Remember the person who died.

- My experience with grieving young people has taught me that remembering the past makes hoping for the future possible.

- The process of beginning to embrace memories often begins with the funeral, which offers an opportunity to remember the person who died and affirm the value of the life that was lived.

- As you reach out to the teen, be alert for creative and spontaneous ways to remember the person who died. Flip through photo albums, tell stories. Journal writing can be particularly helpful for adolescents who may not be ready yet to talk openly about their memories.

- Keep in mind that remembering can be difficult for teens. Some memories are painful, even frightening. But many are joyful and allow the teen to relive the happy times.

Carpe diem

Invite the teen to share a memory of the person who died. Be specific. Ask, "What about that time you and Jill went to soccer camp together?" or "What did your mom used to cook for the holidays?"

6.

UNDERSTAND THE SIX NEEDS OF MOURNING

Need 4: Develop a new self-identity.

- As social beings, we think of ourselves in relation to the people we care about. I'm not just Alan Wolfelt but a son, a brother, a husband, a father. When my father died last year, I was suddenly fatherless.

- Teenagers may be even more closely linked to those around them because their self-identities are just emerging.

- The death of a family member may also require young people to take on roles that had been filled by the person who died. If younger brother Brian always took out the garbage and then he dies, someone still has to take out the garbage. Taking on the new role can be very difficult for the teen survivor.

- No one can "fill in" for the person who died. Don't try to find a substitute father/best friend/grandparent/etc. for the teen, at least not in the early months after the death. Support relationships, yes. Replacements, no!

Carpe diem

Write the teen a note that both honors his old identity and demonstrates allegiance to his new one. For example: "You are a wonderful son and gave your father great joy. You continue to be a unique and special person who means so very much to me and many others."

7.

UNDERSTAND THE SIX
NEEDS OF MOURNING

Need 5: Search for meaning.

- When someone loved dies, we naturally question the meaning and purpose of life.

- Grieving young people may ask "How?" and "Why?" questions about the death of the person they loved. "How did it happen?" or "Why did this happen?" You can help by letting the grieving teen know that these kinds of questions are both normal and important.

- Don't try to answer all the teen's questions about the meaning of life and death. It's OK—even desirable—to admit that you struggle with the same issues and that nobody knows all the answers.

- Teens sometimes act out their search for meaning. Drunk driving and other behaviors that test their mortality are all too common among grieving teens. While in general you shouldn't judge the ways in which the grieving young person searches for meaning, life-threatening behaviors obviously require intervention.

Carpe diem

Ask the teen what she thinks happens after death. Share your beliefs about life and death and spirituality with her without pressuring her to believe what you believe.

8.

UNDERSTAND THE SIX NEEDS OF MOURNING

Need 6: Continue to receive support from adults.

- The last and perhaps most important mourning need for teens is to receive ongoing support from adults.

- Grief is a process, not an event, and grieving young people will continue to need your support for weeks, months and years after the death and the funeral.

- Unfortunately, our society places too much value on "carrying on" and "doing well" after a death. So, many mourners are abandoned by their friends and family soon after the death.

- As they grow and mature developmentally, teens will naturally grieve the death on new and ever deeper levels. I call this "catch-up mourning" (see Idea 9). If you can help the grieving teen mourn as the need arises (even years after the death), you will be helping him grow into a well-adjusted, loving adult.

Carpe diem

Stop for a moment and think: When did the teen's loved one die? Has your support for him waned since the funeral? Has your contact been less and less frequent? Commit right now to contacting or spending time with the teen every week this year.

9.

Know that grief does not proceed in orderly, predictable "stages."

- Though the "Needs of Mourning" (Ideas 3-8) are numbered 1-6, grief is not an orderly progression towards healing. Don't fall into the trap of thinking that the teen's grief journey will be predictable or always forward-moving.

- Usually, grief hurts more before it hurts less.

- The teen will probably encounter a multitude of different emotions in a wave-like fashion. He will also likely encounter more than one need of mourning at the same time.

- Teens often do "catch-up" mourning at developmental milestones. Important events like prom or high school graduation—even when they take place years after the death— may cause the grieving teen to feel particularly sad because the person who died isn't there to share the moment. Many grieving teens will continue to do catch-up mourning as they enter adulthood and reach other milestones like marrying or having children.

Carpe diem

Review the Needs of Mourning (Ideas 3-8). Which one seems most prominent right now in the teen's grief journey? Think of ways you can help the teen work on this need.

10.

DON'T expect the teen to mourn or heal in a certain way or in a certain time.

- The teen's unique grief journey will be shaped by many factors, including:
  - the nature of the relationship he had with the person who died.
  - the age of the person who died.
  - the circumstances of the death.
  - his unique personality.
  - his cultural background.
  - his religious or spiritual beliefs.
  - his gender.
  - his support systems.

- Because of these and other factors, no two deaths are ever mourned in precisely the same way.

- Don't have rigid expectations for the teen's thoughts, feelings and behaviors. Instead, think of your role as one who "walks with," not behind or in front of, the teen.

Carpe diem

Next time you're with the teen, remember to use the "teach me" principle of learning about her grief. If you listen, she will likely teach you about the various influences listed above.

11.

Consider the teen's relationship to the person who died.

- Each teen's response to a death depends largely upon the relationship he had with the person who died.

- For example, teens will naturally grieve differently the deaths of a parent, a classmate and a grandparent.

- The closer the teen felt to the person who died, the more difficult his grief is likely to be. Ambivalent or conflicted relationships can also complicate grief.

- One good way I've found to encourage the teen to teach you about his relationship with the person who died is to ask him to show you photos of the person who died. Relationship themes naturally emerge as the teen describes what's going on in the photos. (Also see Idea 37.)

Carpe diem

Think about the teen's relationship with the person who died—from his point of view. Set aside your own thoughts and feelings and enter into his world as you consider this point.

12.

If a teen's parent has died, consider this:

- The parent-child bond may be the strongest and most significant in life. When this bond is severed by death, the grieving teen needs ample love and support from the other adults in her life.

- Perhaps the most important influence on the teen's grief journey will be the response of the surviving parent or other important adults in the teen's life. While they cannot ignore their own grief and mourning, they must focus as much as possible on helping the teen mourn.

- For the teen, the loss of a parent often results in many additional losses, such as loss of financial stability or loss of a home and neighborhood friends if the family has to move.

Carpe diem

When a teen's parent dies, take care not to send in same-gender "substitutes" right away. Teens are especially resistant to new parent figures. Instead, consider soliciting the help of adults of the opposite gender of the parent who died.

13.

If a teen's sibling has died, consider this:

- Next to the death of a parent, the death of a sibling can be the most traumatic event in a teen's life. Grieving siblings often feel:

  - Guilt. "I wished for John to go away forever and he died" is a common thought among teens who haven't been given the concrete details of the sibling's death and who haven't been assured that they were not at fault.

  - Fear. When a teen's brother or sister dies, another young person has died. So, confronting this reality can mean confronting the possibility of one's own death.

  - Confusion. One 13-year-old girl I counseled after the death of her brother asked me, "Am I still a big sister?" This young person was obviously struggling with the confusing task of redefining herself.

- When a child dies, most of the grief support from family members and friends gets focused on the parents. But what about the surviving siblings? They are often as profoundly impacted by the death as their parents are. And in some ways they are even more deserving of our attention because they are still children.

Carpe diem

Ask a trustworthy adult who is particularly good at relating to the surviving sibling to be "in charge" of helping him in the coming weeks and months. This kind of one-on-one partnership ensures that the teen isn't being neglected while the rest of the family is understandably in turmoil.

14.

Don't expect the teen to take on the role of a parent or sibling who died.

- Sometimes when a family member dies, a teen is expected to assume the responsibilities of the person who died. Such expectations can be unfair or unrealistic and may rob the teen of his own experiences as a teenager. Instead, discuss ways in which other family members and friends can help take on some of the responsibilities once fulfilled by the person who died.

- Never tell a grieving boy—no matter how mature-looking and acting—that he is "the man of the house now." Teenagers are NOT men and should not be expected to be responsible for the family.

- Likewise, grieving girls shouldn't be expected to fill their mother's shoes if the mother dies.

Carpe diem

Assure the teen that even though family life will be different, she can still enjoy her teenage years and her individuality. Let her know that any extra help she offers will be appreciated, but that she shouldn't try to replace the person who died.

15.

If a teen's grandparent has died, consider this:

- When a grandparent has died, the grandchildren may or may not actively mourn; the intensity of their feelings depends on the closeness of the relationship they had with the grandparent who died.

- Sometimes when older people die, we deny or minimize our grief (and that of our children) because "it was time" or "he lived a long, full life." Even when these statements are true, we still need to mourn and so do our children.

- The death of a grandparent or great-grandparent is often the first death a teen experiences. Now is a good time to teach the teen about the importance of funerals and about your spiritual beliefs regarding death as well as model open mourning habits.

Carpe diem

You may have many photos that depict the teen and the grandparent who died together. If so, frame one in a suitable frame and present it as a special gift. Write a few lines that describe what was going on the day of the photo. If you don't have photos of the two together, frame one of the grandparent instead.

16.

If a teen's friend has died, consider this:

- As teenagers naturally separate from their families, they attach more to their peer group. Friends, including boyfriends and girlfriends, may become the teen's most important source of affirmation and acceptance.

- So, if a teen's friend dies, the hurt can be especially painful. This may have been the person he felt closest to and related best to right now in his young life.

- Remember that for a teen, the death of a friend or sibling is the death of another young person. Not only will the teen probably feel despair and outrage at this injustice, but the death can also make the teen aware, perhaps for the first time, that he or she is mortal and will also die someday.

Carpe diem

Encourage the teen to write a letter to the parents of the young person who died telling them how special his friend was to him and why. The letter is a form of mourning. It helps the teen express his feelings and it will be cherished by the parents.

17.

Acknowledge grief stemming from the loss of a pet.

- Losing a pet may be the teen's first encounter with the death of someone she loves. Her pet may have been her closest friend and confidante. The two of them may have been together since they were both very young. Maybe they even slept together.

- The grief a teen may experience over losing a pet can be as real and powerful as that of losing a person. Let the teen know you're sorry about her loss. Give her permission to grieve.

- Don't suggest getting another pet right away. Give the teen some time and space to integrate the loss first.

Carpe diem

Give the teen a small journal in which she can write about her pet—memories of their times together, feelings about the pet being gone, letters to the pet. She can also include photos of her pet in the journal.

18.

Consider the nature of the death.

- Was the death sudden or anticipated? How old was the person who died? Was this death stigmatized (e.g. deaths from suicide, homicide or AIDs)? Deaths of young people, violent deaths and stigmatized deaths tend to complicate grief for all survivors, young and old.

- The more sudden the death, the more likely the teen is to mourn in "doses" and push away some of the pain at first.

- If the death was due to a terminal illness, don't assume that the teen has anticipated the death. Parents and other well-intentioned but misguided adults sometimes aren't honest about the illness; they keep the truth from teenagers in an attempt to protect them. In these cases, what looks to the outside world like an anticipated death is really a sudden and unexpected death to the teen.

- Teens who have been involved in and aware of a terminal illness are not done mourning when the death occurs. They may feel relief at first but other difficult thoughts and emotions will surface in the coming weeks and months.

Carpe diem

If you don't know all the details of the death, inform yourself about them today. That way you'll better understand the teen's grief and be able to help him mourn in appropriate ways.

19.

If the death was violent, consider this:

- Following a violent death, the teen may well feel total disbelief and numbness. It is normal for teens not to function in the early days after a violent act.

- Open, brutally honest communication is necessary at a time like this. Do not attempt to protect the teen by hiding or sugar-coating the truth. He'll likely hear all the gory details elsewhere anyway.

- Support groups and individual counseling are often worthwhile precautions in cases like this. Even if the teen seems to be "doing well," make sure he has ample opportunity to express his feelings and confront the demons within.

- Focus the teen's natural rage on activism in the months after the death. Help him get involved in school and community groups that help prevent this type of tragedy from happening again. He can also work to memorialize the victims.

Carpe diem

If this death affected the teen's entire circle of friends, get all the parents together, as well as other concerned adults, and create an action plan for helping the kids through this extraordinarily difficult time. Promise to keep an eye on each other's children and work for the good of the entire group.

20.

Think about the teen's cultural or ethnic background.

- The grieving teen's response to death is influenced by her cultural and ethnic backgrounds. Different cultures are known for the various ways they express (or repress) their grief.

- Cultures that encourage outward expressions of grief are more likely to instill healthy mourning practices in grieving teens.

- Mourning-avoiding cultures, on the other hand, like those prevalent in North American society today, often make a teen's grief journey more difficult.

- Whatever the teen's cultural or ethnic background, be respectful of its customs and beliefs.

Carpe diem

Think about your own cultural or ethnic background.
How has it influenced your grief and mourning? Then
ask yourself: How can I stay sensitive to and respectful of
this teen's unique cultural and ethnic background?

21.

Talk about death.

- Death is a fact of life, yet people are often reluctant to confront death and talk about it openly. But talking about death in general is one way to help dissipate feelings of fear or horror and move towards accepting death as one more stage in the journey of life.

- Knowing that we're all going to die someday can make us more fully appreciate and value our own life and all the lives around us. It's also what drives us to make the most of life while we can.

- Take advantage of everyday opportunities to talk about death—the death of a pet, the death of a sports star, deaths due to natural disasters or wars.

Carpe diem

Initiate a discussion about death with the teen. Refer to the cycles of nature or to different cultural and religious beliefs about dying. Ask the teen to talk about his own beliefs about both life and death.

22.

Establish trust and confidentiality. Then honor it.

- Getting a teen to talk about his thoughts and feelings can be one of the most important activities you can engage him in. He's more likely to share this personal side of himself with someone he knows will listen in confidence and without passing judgment.

- Unless you are already very close to the grieving teen, building trust may take time. Talk with him regularly and try to spend time with him often. Be there.

- If the teen shares his private thoughts and feelings with you, do not share them with anyone else UNLESS you are afraid the teen might harm himself or others.

Carpe diem

Assure the teen that you care and want to help, and that he can be open with you. Let him know you want to see him reconcile his loss and be happy again. Promise your confidentiality.

23.

Listen without judging.

- The most important gift you can give a grieving teen is the gift of your presence. Be there for him. Initiate contact. And listen, listen, listen.

- Listen some more. If he's the type of teen who wants to talk about the death over and over again, listen patiently each time. Telling and retelling the story helps mourners accommodate the loss.

- Don't worry so much about what you will say in return; instead, concentrate on the words being shared with you.

- Often, teens don't communicate very well or talk very much, especially to adults. So when he does talk, listen especially carefully. If he starts to open up to you and you are distracted or butt in or judge what he is telling you, you have closed a window of opportunity that may never open again.

Carpe diem

If you want the teen to talk to you, don't sit him down on the sofa next to you and ask him what's on his mind. Instead, go for a hike together or play street hockey or build a half-pipe—DO something together and conversation may naturally unfold.

24.

Respect the teen's wish not to talk about the death.

- While the six needs of mourning are common to most people, each individual grieves in her own unique way and not according to any particular schedule. Talking about the death can be helpful, but pushing the teen to talk about it when she's not ready can cause more harm than good. Let the teen open up in her own way when she's ready.

- Some teens, because of their strong need to separate from adults, will never want to talk about the death—at least not to you. If this is the case, try to find other outlets for the teen's grief, such as teen support groups, journaling, and artwork.

- By showing compassion, not forcing the issue, and being a good listener, you show the teen that you care and will honor his wish to grieve on his own terms.

Carpe diem

Go with the teen to a park, restaurant, or other relaxing setting, and talk about things other than the death. Once the teen talks to you about other things, she may begin to open up about the death.

25.

Pay attention to your nonverbal communication.

- At least half of the art of listening and "being there" for the teen involves nonverbal communication.

- Are you looking at the teen when she talks to you? Looking away or distracting yourself with busywork while she's talking communicates that you're either really not listening or uncomfortable with listening.

- Lean into the teen. Nod your head. Keep an open posture. Don't cross your arms in front of your chest.

- For teens who are especially resistant to adult help, you may want to ignore this advice and be more nonchalant and less focused on her when you try to talk with her. While she's sitting at the kitchen table doing homework, for example, instead of sitting down across from her and trying to strike up a conversation, busy yourself preparing dinner at the counter. Look at the food instead of her. Keep your distance. These techniques may make her feel less threatened and therefore more open to communication.

Carpe diem

Today, note which nonverbal communication style seems to work better with this teen: focused and close or unfocused and farther away. Use this information to your advantage from now on.

26.

DON'T fall back on clichés.

- A teen's deep and extremely complicated feelings of loss are often dismissed with overly simple, empty phrases such as:
  - Give it time.
  - Keep busy.
  - Be strong.
  - At least he didn't suffer.
  - You're young; you'll get over this.
  - She lived a long life.
  - Try not to think about it.
  - You'll become stronger because of this.
  - Be glad you had him as long as you did.
  - She wouldn't have wanted you to be sad.
  - Life is for the living.

- Though well-intended, such clichés hurt because they diminish the teen's feelings and take away her right—and need—to mourn.

Carpe diem

Read Idea 28 right now. That way you'll be better equipped to talk to the teen next time you meet.

27.

DON'T use religious clichés, either.

- Sometimes people use theologized clichés in an attempt to comfort:
  - It was God's will.
  - God only gives you what you can handle.
  - Now she's in a better place.
  - This is a blessing.
  - Now you have an angel in heaven.

- Like other clichés, these expressions tend to minimize the mourner's loss and need to mourn.

- Even if the teen comes from a religious background and has faith, he still needs to mourn this death.

Carpe diem

If you've used any of the phrases on this page or the page before, don't worry too much. The teen knows you are trying to help him. But do make an effort from this day forward not to fall back on clichés again as you attempt to help a teen in grief.

28.

Do say this.

- I'm sorry.

- I'm thinking of you.

- I care.

- I love you.

- You are so important to me.

- I'm here for you.

- I want to help.

- I'm thinking of you and praying for you every day.

- I want you to know I loved _____, too.

Carpe diem

Send the teen an e-mail that says, "I just want you to
know I care about you and am here for you."

29.

Use the name of the person who died.

- When you're talking to the teen, don't avoid using the name of the person who died. Avoiding it diminishes the loss.

- Instead, acknowledge the significance of the death by talking about the person who died: "I remember when David...", "When did your mom first get sick?", "I thought of Laura today because..."

- Using the name of the person who died personalizes your concern and expresses your willingness to honor the "telling of the story."

Carpe diem

Look up the name of the person who died in a baby book and jot down its meaning. If appropriate, write a note explaining this meaning to the teen and why it seems fitting to you.

30.

Call the teen.

- Many people avoid contact with someone who is grieving. The painful and personal nature of grief and our own fears about death may interfere with our desire to help. Too, we may feel that anything we say or do won't be adequate, since we can't bring the dead person back to life.

- But personal contact helps to reaffirm life and develop the teen's understanding that there are others in the world and that, with their support, she can survive even the most difficult times.

- A gesture as simple as a phone call can help assure the teen that she is not alone and someone else cares.

Carpe diem

Right now, call the teen, if only to let her know that you're thinking of her and wanted her to know.

31.

Write a letter.

- Writing a letter is a different kind of way to express yourself. It allows you to think about what you want to convey and choose just the right words to say it. Because writing a letter often takes more time and effort than a conversation, a handwritten letter is often viewed as a gift—especially these days when the personal letter has almost become a lost art.

- Letters are precious, and people often save letters that mean a lot to them. The teen may enjoy reading your letter over and over again.

- Some ideas for starting your letter:

    - "I wanted to let you know that..."

    - "I'm so sorry that..."

    - "You're very special to me because..."

    - "What I remember most about _____ (the person who died) is..."

Carpe diem

Pick up a "Just Thinking of You" card or an attractive piece of stationery or handmade paper, and write a letter to the teen. Let him know that you care and you're there for him.

32.

Attend the funeral.

- Funerals are our way of saying goodbye to the person who died and honoring the life that was lived. They are also our way of demonstrating our support for those most impacted by the death.

- Even if you didn't personally know the person who died, it's appropriate for you to attend the funeral to show your support for the teen.

- Try hard to attend all phases of the funeral—the visitation, the funeral service, the committal and the gathering afterwards.

Carpe diem

Ask the teen about the funeral experience. Sometimes latent questions or fears or regrets will surface about what did or didn't happen at the funeral, and giving voice to them can help tremendously.

33.

Have the teen write an epitaph for the person who died.

- It can be difficult to express that quality or aspect that we feel best commemorates the person who died. But that's exactly what an epitaph strives to do.

- The teen may not have been involved in creating the epitaph for the person who died. That doesn't mean she can't write one now. The act of focusing on those qualities the teen cherished most in the person who died calls for concentration and precision in choosing the right words. The process of writing gives the teen another opportunity to begin to shift relationship from one of presence to one of memory —and the epitaph itself becomes another memento.

Carpe diem

Initiate with the teen a discussion about epitaphs. Perhaps give examples of some that have struck you in one way or another. Suggest that the teen compose her own epitaph to the person who died. Write one yourself based on what you know. Read aloud what you've written.

34.

Help the teen choose a keepsake.

- Following a death, survivors are faced with the task of sorting through and disposing of the belongings of the person who died. Young people should be included in this process when possible.

- Ask the teen if he would like to keep anything that belonged to the person who died. If the person who died was especially significant in his young life, you may want to box up other items and save them for appropriate times later in the teen's life.

- Sometimes keepsakes can be stored in a "memory box" (see Idea 81) created especially for the teen.

Carpe diem

Today, talk to the teen about keepsakes. If he has already selected some, ask him about their significance. If he hasn't, help him make a plan for choosing and procuring at least one.

35.

Give the teen permission to find comfort in "linking objects."

- "Linking objects" are simply items that belonged to the person who died in which the teen takes comfort. They offer him a physical "link" to the person who died.

- You may want to give the teen a special linking object—maybe something she can wear like an article of clothing or a piece of jewelry.

- Other appropriate linking objects for teens include books, knick-knacks, artwork, sports gear, games, or CDs.

- The teen's natural defiance may make her say she doesn't want any of this "junk." If that's her attitude, fine; don't push. But do box something up for a time in the future when she may find the item very meaningful.

Carpe diem

Buy a shadow box—a special deep frame designed to hold mementos—and help the teen create a display of linking objects for her room.

36.

Allow the teen to cry.

- Tears are a natural cleansing and healing mechanism. It's OK to cry. In fact, it's good to cry when you feel like it. Plus, tears are a form of mourning. They are sacred!

- Many people are uncomfortable when others cry in their presence. For the teen's sake, try not to be one of those people.

- If the teen cries when you're with her, resist the urge to hand her a tissue or hug her right away. Though loving and well-intended, both of these gestures tend to send the message that you'd like her to stop crying.

- Instead, lean into her and simply be present. Of course, if you sense that she wants your touch, by all means hold her hand or give her a hug.

- Of course, many teens—especially boys—will fight the urge to cry because they have been conditioned to believe that tears are a sign of weakness. Dispel this myth through modeling; cry in the teen's presence when you feel like crying.

Carpe diem

Box up a linen handkerchief for the teen and present it with a
note that explains why crying is good for people in grief.

37.

Ask to see photos.

- Maybe you didn't know the person who died, or maybe you weren't as close to her as the teen was. You can better understand the teen's feelings—and help him recall happier times—by asking him to share with you photos of the person who died.

- The teen may be reluctant to talk about the person who died, but when he shows you photos, he may reveal things about the more memorable moments they spent together.

Carpe diem

Ask the teen if he has photos of the person who died,
and if so, would he mind sharing them with you.

38.

Mourn together.

- Mourning is the outward expression of grief and is important for reconciliation to take place. Regardless of whether or not you knew the person who died, you can provide empathy and support to the teen by mourning with him.

- Wearing dark clothing, flying a flag at half mast, and attending a funeral, memorial service, or burial for the person who died are some of the more conventional ways that people mourn death in this country.

- While inherently sad, mourning doesn't have to be all doom and gloom. Some cultures and religions mourn by having parties—singing, dancing, and laughing to celebrate the life of the person who died and the belief that he's gone to a better place.

Carpe diem

Together, brainstorm ways in which the two of you—and perhaps others, as well—could let the world know you're in mourning. Make armbands, wear photo buttons or sew a symbol to your jackets.

39.

Be compassionate.

- You probably wouldn't be helping a grieving teen if you weren't compassionate, but even we caregiver types can use a refresher course in compassion now and then.

- Compassion grows from empathy, which involves projecting ourselves into the teen's world and viewing the situation through the teen's eyes.

- To have empathy also is to understand the meaning of the teen's experience instead of imposing meaning on that experience from the outside.

- Empathy is about a desire to understand and an awareness that you can't "fix" the pain of grief. Acting on your empathy is being compassionate.

Carpe diem

Compassionate literally means "with passion." Care
for this teen "with passion" today.

40.

Be genuine.

- You can't really help the grieving teen unless you can be genuine with her. Young people can smell a phony a mile away.

- Be yourself. Be honest. Be sincere.

- You don't have to be good at everything (or the kind of person who could pull off all the suggestions in this book) to help the grieving teen; you just need to help in ways that feel comfortable for you.

- If you don't relate particularly well to teens, that's OK. Relating to teens can be really tough! You can still help by writing letters to the teen, giving small gifts and galvanizing the other adults in the teen's life.

Carpe diem

What are you good at? What are you not so good at? An honest assessment of your strengths and weaknesses will help you decide how best you can help this teenager.

41.

Be the teen's advocate.

- Think of yourself as the grieving teen's advocate. Even if you aren't around him all the time, you can still take steps to ensure that his other environments are supportive and loving.

- Sometimes a few simple phone calls is all it takes to alert adults in the teen's life to his special needs right now.

- Consider the following spheres of influence: immediate family, extended family, neighborhood, school, circle of friends, extracurricular activities and church/place of worship.

- Don't abuse the teen's trust by disclosing information he has asked you to keep private. Let the teen know you've talked to these people so he won't be taken caught off guard when they bring up the subject.

Carpe diem

Write thank you notes to all the adults who are helping this teen right now. If you affirm their support, it will likely continue.

42.

Let the teen be a teen.

- When a teen loses someone special, adults often expect the teen to behave in a stoic, adult-like way. "Be strong." "Grow up." "Don't be a crybaby." These are some of the messages peers and adults often send to teens, sometimes without even realizing it. While they may be well-intended, such comments may be interpreted by the teen as cruel or insensitive, or may lead the teen to avoid the pain of grief.

- Teens are still kids. While their changing outward appearance can make them look like grown-up men and women, they're still immature inside.

- Let this teen be a teen and do all the normal things teens do—hang out with his friends, sleep late, wear weird clothing, rebel. Be considerate of his "schedule" when trying to fit in time with him.

Carpe diem

You can help a teen during this difficult time by doing something as simple as giving him permission to mourn. Let him know the emotions he's feeling are normal, and that experiencing and expressing them are important for healing and growth.

43.

Offer help from the community.

- Most communities have public and private resources for helping people through difficult situations. Counselors, hospices, funeral homes, phone help lines, and library resources are just some of the places a person who's grieving can turn for help.

- Even if the teen chooses not to use such resources, just knowing that they're there can be a tremendous comfort.

Carpe diem

Make a list of grief and counseling resources within your community, including the name, location, telephone number, and a brief discussion of the services provided and cost, if any. Give this list to the teen, and let him know these people are there for him.

44.

Inquire about support groups.

- Grief support groups are a safe place for teens to express their thoughts and feelings with peers who've also had someone loved die.

- Sharing similar experiences with other teenagers may help this teen feel like she's not alone and she's not "weird."

- Your local hospice or funeral home may offer a free or low-cost support group for teens.

- If the death was recent, the teen may not be ready for a support group. Many mourners are more open to joining a support group several months after the death. On the other hand, some teens may want to attend a support group right away. This is fine. Never tell them "it's too soon" if they feel ready.

Carpe diem

Call around today and get a support group schedule for the teen. Give it to her non-confrontationally; don't insist that she join a group but rather suggest she might be interested in one. Offer to help sign her up and drive her there and back if needs that type of assistance.

45.

Galvanize the teen's support network.

- As much as you care about the bereaved teen, you can't expect yourself to be his sole source of emotional support. Sharing the work of grief support with others who also care about the teen will give him a variety of people he can contact when he might need or want company or help.

- Bring adults who care about the teen together to brainstorm ways you can assist the teen now and in the months to follow.

- Don't forget teachers, coaches, religious leaders, neighbors, relatives, family friends—anyone whom the teen respects and trusts.

Carpe diem

Ask the teen for the names of the most important people in his life. Make a list of those people and contact them about forming a support system. Then meet to discuss different ideas for helping the teen and one another.

46.

Ease the teen's relationships with her peers.

- Teens can be tough on other teens, especially when they sense a weak spot or difference. Grief can create such a difference.

- Talk to the grieving teen about her friendships. Ask her if her friends are being supportive or if they're acting weird. Make some suggestions for talking to them about the death.

- Have one of the teen's teachers or friends' parents talk to her friends about the death and how they can help.

- Invite some friends over to the grieving teen's house and help make it a fun time. Or take them all on an outing together and supervise, modeling open and positive communication.

Carpe diem

Ask the teen if she'd like to have a party or outing for her and her friends. If she's interested, offer to help plan it and chaperone.

47.

Help the teen's family mourn.

- The family's response to the death will play a crucial role in the teen's mourning and integration of the loss.

- If the family is open and loving even in the face of death, the teen will probably be taught how and encouraged to mourn.

- If the family doesn't talk about death and tends to repress feelings, the teen will have a hard time mourning in their presence.

- If appropriate, talk to the teen's parents or primary caregivers about their grief. Encourage them to talk about the death as a family. Help the family and you'll be helping the teen.

Carpe diem

Observe the mourning style of the teen's family. Gently suggest family counseling if you think it would help.

48.

Visit the grave or scattering site together.

- If the person who died was buried, ask the teen if you can go together to visit the grave.

- Visiting the burial site helps the teen to accept the reality of the death and know that if she ever wants a quiet moment with the one she lost, she can always come here to speak to the person, say a prayer, or just spend time reflecting.

- If the person who died was cremated, perhaps you can visit the columbarium or scattering site with the teen.

Carpe diem

On a nice day, accompany the teen to the grave. Where is it placed? What does the headstone say? Are there flowers and trees nearby? Affirming the material things associated with the person who died helps keep the memory of that person alive.

49.

Visit a pet store.

- It's hard to go into a pet store and not come out smiling. Kittens tumble over each other. Puppies jump up and fall down. Hamsters and gerbils run in circles. Snakes slide around. Parakeets chirp. Mackaws squawk, sometimes talk, maybe even perch on your hand. Fish cruise by in kaleidoscopic colors and patterns.

- Pet stores remind us of the diversity of life in this crazy world, and of the wonder of birth and growing up.

- Teens who can't have a pet of their own but love animals can volunteer at the local animal shelter or walk neighborhood dogs as a part-time job.

Carpe diem

Accompany the teen to a pet store. Ask him about his own pet. If he doesn't have a pet and could get one, what kind would he like to have, and why?

50.

Spend time with younger kids.

- What is it about children that so often brings a smile to our face? They ask for little but give much through their spontaneity, playfulness and candor, and through the innocent way they view the world.

- Being in a child's presence brings a renewed appreciation of life. It also helps us recall that time in our own lives when we weren't weighed down with responsibilities or knowledge about the sadness that exists in the world.

- If the teen enjoys children but doesn't get to spend much time around them, arrange for her to babysit. Pair her up with a same-gender child who needs attention and ask the teen to act as mentor.

Carpe diem

Invite the teen to join you on a visit to a children's ward in a nearby hospital. Let her know the children will appreciate her visit.

51.

Contemplate the universe.

- Stargazing is a relaxing, renewing activity that's perfect for many grieving teens. The darkness and the solitude and the heavens foster frank conversation about the meaning of life and death.

- Do you have a telescope? If so, get it out and refresh your memory about how to use it. If not, gazing at the night sky with the naked eye is just as awe-inspiring.

- Invite the teen for a drive in the country where city lights won't obscure the starlight. Bring chaise lawn chairs or a couple of blankets so you can lie on your backs and watch in comfort.

- Visit your local planetarium for the next best thing.

Carpe diem

Call your local extension office or visit your local library and determine when the next meteor shower is. Invite the teen to accompany you to a good viewing spot and stay up late watching the show.

52.

Talk with the teen about heaven.

- Depending on the teen's spiritual upbringing, he may or may not believe in "heaven" per se, but he probably has some thoughts and feelings about what happens after death.

- Be his sounding board on this important issue. If he has doubts or fears, help him express them.

- If the teen's faith teaches him that afterlife is a certainty, ask him what he thinks the afterlife is like.

- Some religions emphasize that death should be an event of celebration because it leads to eternal life. Even if the teen believes this to be true, he still needs to mourn and embrace his painful feelings.

Carpe diem

Encourage the teen to write a poem about or paint a picture of heaven and what he sees the person who died doing there.

53.

Get cultured.

- Accompanying the teen to a cultural event can be fun, entertaining, educational, or all of the above. Invite the teen to a movie, play, concert, art show, or reading, and give him the opportunity to enter a new environment and a new state of mind.

- Cultural activities explore the human experience, and may offer interpretations or messages that will help the teen reassess the way he looks at life. Even if what you attend is just plain silly, the laughter alone can remind him of the happiness of being alive.

Carpe diem

Search the local paper, museums, schools, galleries, and universities for cultural activities now taking place. Choose one or two that you think will appeal to the teen. Then call him and ask him to join you.

54.

Tickle a funny bone.

- Be on the lookout for ways you can lighten the mood, when appropriate. Laughter helps lift the heavy feelings that come with grieving. It's also a great tension reliever.

- Make a point of remembering a joke you like and share it with the teen. Check out new comedy movies and videos, as well as live comedy and improv shows in your area, and make a date for an evening of humor. And don't forget to look on the web, where you can get ideas from sites like jokes.com and laugh-of-the-day.com

Carpe diem

Take the teen to a toy store and check out the wind-up toys on display.

55.

Treat the teen to a neck and shoulder massage.

- Our necks and shoulders are common places to store stress. We use these parts of our bodies in virtually every activity we do, and at night we sometimes unintentionally damage them by sleeping in weird positions or on poor mattresses or pillows.

- A number of certified massage therapists offer 15-minute neck-and-shoulder massages. The person getting the massage sits in a chair that's designed to support the head while the therapist stands behind and works the muscles in the neck and shoulders.

- A short, professional massage can go a long way toward relieving physical, mental, and emotional stress.

Carpe diem

Check the yellow pages for certified massage therapists, and call to find out which do chair massages. Give the teen a gift certificate for one, or ask her to go along with you to get one.

56.

Play a game.

- Games can involve strategy, creativity, concentration, and skill. Or they can be just plain silly.

- One of the great things about games is they take your mind off other things. At the same time, you're having fun, socializing, and developing skills.

- Having the teen play games with younger kids is a nice way to retreat to the carefree world of childhood. Suggest playing Candyland or Chutes and Ladders with a preschooler.

Carpe diem

Engage the teen in a game of cards, Pictionary, Scrabble, Monopoly, dominoes, Life, Battleship, cribbage, chess, or other game he enjoys. Invite others to join in a group game.

57.

Light the night.

- Light is illuminating. It helps us see our way. It represents hope. It's the sign of a new day. Darkness can be just the opposite. It obstructs our vision and sometimes makes us feel afraid or hopeless. But even a small light can help dispel those fears.

- Give the teen a nightlight to help light up the darkness. The soft light it emanates can be comforting, like a beacon in the night.

- In addition to nightlights that mount right in the electric socket, consider lava lamps, lit globes, neon signs and other teen-friendly types of lighting.

Carpe diem

Go nightlight shopping. You can find them in all varieties, made from stained glass, ceramic, seashells, pressed dried flowers, and more. Pick out one you think the teen will like and give it to her with a wish for peaceful nights.

58.

Move to the music.

- Music moves us. Whether it's rock, ska, jazz, hip-hop, country, classical, funk, instrumental, or a cappella, music has the ability to rock, soothe, energize, or relax. It seems to touch our very core, whether we're playing the music, listening to it, or dancing to it.

- Take the teen to a music store and buy her that new CD she's been wanting or give her an iTunes gift card.

- Get tickets to a local concert; pick something neither you nor the teen has ever attended before.

Carpe diem

Many coffee houses feature musicians, especially on Friday and Saturday nights. Take the teen out for a café mocha and an evening of music.

59.

Offer to pick up homework assignments.

- Because of her loss, the teen may miss several days or even a week or more of school. Falling behind in schoolwork can make it difficult for her to catch up and may nudge feelings of being overwhelmed into the realm of despair. If her grades begin to fall, she may lose hope that she'll ever get back on track.

- If you're a classmate, offer to make notes of the day's activities in each of the teen's classes, and pass those notes along to the teen. If you're a teacher, advocate for the teen. Talk with all her teachers and suggest easing some of her load right now.

- Talk to the teen's parents about giving her permission to let her schoolwork slide a bit for now. It's normal—even desirable—for the teen to focus on grief and mourning for a time before she can start concentrating on school again.

Carpe diem

Pick up homework assignments and deliver them to the teen. Offer to help with homework. Coordinate with others to plan a "catch-up-with-schoolwork" party.

60.

Do a project together.

- What makes this teen's clock tick? Think about her interests then invite her to do a project with you.

- Pick something you can complete in an afternoon or, even better, something the two of you can work on together in the coming weeks and months. This will give her a goal to work towards and a regular activity to look forward to.

- Some ideas: build a bookcase or CD tower for the teen's room; restore an old car; make a quilt; plant a garden; put together a 2,000 piece puzzle; paint and decorate her room.

Carpe diem

Plan a project the two of you can work on next time you're together.

61.

Teach the teen something new.

- Is there something the teen has always wanted to learn how to do? Ask her.

- If she's interested, teach her something you're good at. When she loses interest it's time to move on.

- Enroll the teen in a special class or hire a private instructor for a month or two if she's really serious about a particular endeavor. Focusing on this new activity may help her balance the happy and the sad in her life right now.

- Maybe both of you can learn to do something that person who died liked to do.

Carpe diem

Ask the teen to make a list of 10 things she'd like to learn how to do. Together, pick one thing and make it a reality!

62.

Make a collage together.

- Invite the teen to make a collage about the person who died or about things he'd like to do in his lifetime. Both themes will give him opportunities to focus on important mourning needs: remembering the person who died and looking toward the future.

- Work on a collage of your own as well.

- As you cut out images for your collage and arrange them on your board, talk about their significance to your theme and ask the teen to talk about his.

Carpe diem

Gather poster board or foam core, a glue stick or some rubber cement, a stack of old magazines, a couple pairs of scissors. Then get together for an afternoon or evening of cutting and pasting and creating something you can hang up at home and enjoy again.

63.

Finger-paint.

- Think of things you can do to help the teen have fun again. Remember those art projects we did as kids? They were probably some of the funnest, most creative, and most uninhibited times of our lives—when worries were few and joy in living was abundant.

- An art project like finger-painting can help bring back that carefree state of mind, and also let the teen express herself without using words.

- Similar ideas include making macaroni necklaces, potato stampings, leaf rubbings and pipe cleaner sculptures.

Carpe diem

Organize a finger-painting party with the teen and some of her friends. Supply butcher paper, finger paints, and a place to work. Hang the paintings around the room. Have the artists describe what they see in each painting.

64.

Exercise together.

- Besides keeping the body toned, flexible, and strong, exercise also releases endorphins, or "feel-good" chemicals, in the brain. It's a fact that exercise, especially when done on a regular basis, promotes a sense of well-being.

- Excellent results come from exercising 20-30 minutes a day, five days a week. Exercising all at one time or breaking it up into smaller increments throughout the day yields the same benefits. Having a regular partner can make exercise easier to do—and more fun.

- Get the teen moving by throwing a football, kicking a soccer ball, dancing, skiing, shooting hoops, jogging, riding bikes, playing tennis, training for an athletic event, or walking for a cause. I do Tae Bo with my own teenage daughter and it is great bonding time.

Carpe diem

Is there a certain sport the teen already enjoys, perhaps rollerblading or swimming or tennis? Ask her to teach you to how play.

65.

Imagine what the person who died would do or say.

- If the grieving teen is struggling with a decision or issue, ask her what the person who died would do or say.

- The teen can imagine the person is still alive or the person is giving advice from heaven.

- Sometimes this leads to an anecdote or discussion of the person's life. Sometimes this gives the teen a new perspective on the issue.

- Either way, it's mourning and it will help her!

Carpe diem

Bring up a recent achievement in the teen's life and ask her what the person who died would have done or said. Talking about how proud and happy the person would have been may make her feel sad but will also affirm the relationship she had with this person.

66.

Ask about a parting gift.

- Often, it isn't until after someone's gone that we think about something we wish we'd done before that person died.

- It's never too late to talk about those wishes, however. We can express our feelings and intentions by talking about gifts we would have liked to have given. Whether those gifts are wise or hopeful words, pledges, expressions of love, or material items that hold a special significance, the act of naming them—and the intent behind them—is a way of giving and a way of mourning.

- Such gifts-of-the-heart can still be given to those who live. Suggest that the teen give something to or do something special for a loved one who's still here to appreciate it.

Carpe diem

Ask the teen: If you could, what parting gift would
you have given to the person who died?

67.

Ask a favor.

- Asking the teen to do something for you may not sound like a way of helping, but it is.

- Involving the teen in a productive activity can actually help lighten the load of grief—while also rewarding her with a sense of accomplishment.

- By tending to the needs of someone else, she may also realize and feel good about the fact that she's valued and needed.

- In addition, working together makes the chore more fun and helps to temporarily redirect the teen's focus away from the past and toward the present and the future. Washing cars with my own teenage daughter has proved to be a great way to spend time together.

Carpe diem

Ask the teen to help you with a project at home, such as painting, cleaning, organizing, or holding a garage sale.

68.

Volunteer with the teen.

- Volunteerism is a way of promoting self-worth and a sense of purpose.

- Most communities have lots of volunteer opportunities for teens, especially when adults are willing to help.

- Call your area United Way and ask if there's a local nonprofit or upcoming event in need of two extra pairs of hands. Explain that you and the teen want to work together. Serve meals at a homeless shelter or participate in a roadside trash clean-up.

- Look into volunteer opportunities that have to do with the person who died. If the death was caused by a drunk driver, for example, participate in an area MADD rally. If the person died of cancer, collect money for the American Cancer Society.

Carpe diem

Check the local newspaper for calls for volunteers. Plan a volunteer activity for you and the teen to do together.

69.

Reaffirm life.

- With loss sometimes comes a period of dwelling on the dark side. A teen who's grieving the death of someone he loved may find his thoughts lingering on unanswerable questions about life and death. He may consider life to be futile since everyone eventually dies anyway.

- As people work to accommodate difficult life experiences, they often discover it's not the final destination but the journey that brings meaning and joy to each individual life.

- Life-affirming activities include gardening, volunteering, spending time in nature, playing with little kids.

Carpe diem

Let the teen know how glad you are that he's alive. Tell him what he brings to your life. If he won't tolerate such a personal conversation face-to-face, write him a long, heartfelt letter.

70.

Break bread; share fruit.

- One way to spend some time with the teen AND make sure she gets in some small, healthy meals is to bring some bread and fruit along when you next get together.

- High-fiber breads and crackers, crunchy fruits like apples and pears, or grapes and dried fruits make for tasty snacks that are relatively low in calories but high in vitamins and minerals. Add some chilled bottled water or juice to wash everything down.

- Stopping by your local juice bar for a fruit smoothie is both a fun and healthy outing.

Carpe diem

Fill a small bag or basket with a healthy snack, then take
the teen on a simple outing. If the weather's crummy,
spread a blanket and have an indoor picnic together.

71.

Bring a meal over, or take the teen out to eat.

- One tradition that has survived despite our mourning-avoiding culture is that of bringing a meal to a family who has lost one of its members. The family is often so overwhelmed with grief and making memorial arrangements that they may forget about eating or lose the desire to eat.

- With a teen this problem is compounded by his body's tremendous need for calories and a balanced diet. Yet many teens eat fast foods many days, and when their lives become complicated by a loss, they may stop doing even that.

- What are the teen's favorite healthy snack foods? Be sure to keep them in ample supply during this time.

Carpe diem

Prepare a meal for the teen and his family and bring it to their house, or invite the teen out to a nearby restaurant that offers healthy and tasty food choices.

72.

Cook something together.

- Teens usually don't like to cook when it's presented as a chore, but when they're enthusiastically invited to help prepare a special meal or treat, they'll sometimes join in.

- Pass along a favorite recipe to the teen. Help her prepare it then sit down and enjoy it together!

- Cook a meal for someone who would appreciate it, perhaps a busy mom or a lonely neighbor.

- Enroll the teen in your own little cooking school. Teach her how to cook omelets the first week, roast chicken the next, then spaghetti, etc. She'll learn how to cook, you'll have fun together and over time she'll probably open up about her grief.

Carpe diem

What's the teen's favorite dessert? Buy the ingredients and help her prepare it tonight.

73.

Go bowling.

- Bowling is something just about everyone can do, and it's an activity you can enjoy day or night. The sport calls for strength, balance, concentration, and coordination of body movements. When you pull your arm back, walk toward the pins, and send the ball spinning toward the spot you hope will result in a strike, you become fully immersed in the moment.

- Then there is the thunder of the pins, the sweeping of the pin-clearing machine, the reaction of teammates, and the chance to try again.

- Some bowling alleys have "bowling in the dark"—times when the alley is dimly lit or lit with black lights and the pins, balls and other items glow. Perfect for teens.

Carpe diem

Invite the teen bowling. See if some of her friends want to come along. Create teams and compete for a prize. Or just play for fun.

74.

Go surfing.

- You don't have to be a Web wizard to tap into the wealth of grief information available on the Internet. Even the most basic search will put you in touch with websites that describe grief and offer suggestions for the bereaved and others who wish to be of help.

- Begin your search with the key words "teens" and "grief." Try www. beliefnet.com and www.dougy.org.

- Remember that grieving teens are especially vulnerable and could inadvertently get involved in inappropriate online chat rooms or e-mail relationships. Be sure someone's supervising.

Carpe diem

Provide the teen with a list of helpful websites you've already viewed, or join him at the computer and surf together. Suggest how the teen can use the web to seek information on those topics foremost on his mind.

75.

Go someplace peaceful.

- Where's the most peaceful place you've ever been, and what did it feel like being in that place? Did your concerns seem to melt away? Were you comfortable just being you and just being there at that moment? Did you believe that everything would be OK?

- Different environments can have a big impact on our moods. Places that are closed in, stifling, and manmade can create a feeling of entrapment. Places indoors or out that are aesthetically pleasing and doused with natural light can be uplifting.

- Water elements, such as streams and fountains, also can provide a sense of well-being.

Carpe diem

Take the teen to a park, beach, walking trail, sculpture garden, mountain or other scenic place. Enjoy the feeling of just being there. Pay attention to the sights, sounds, smells, and feel of the area. Let the environment work its magic.

76.

Go buy the book.

- You'll find many good books on mourning and grief at local bookstores and libraries. While you won't find many written specifically for teens, some books for adult mourners are fitting for older teens.

- Grief journals can be especially helpful for grieving teens.

- Poetry, religious texts, even novels about loss may be appropriate for some teens.

- Check out *Chicken Soup for the Teenage Soul* or *The 7 Habits of Highly Effective Teens*.

Carpe diem

Healing Your Grieving Heart for Teens: 100 Practical Ideas is directed at teens themselves and is available through your local bookstore or directly from Companion Press. Call 970/226-6050 or visit www.centerforloss.com to order.

77.

Give a calling card.

- Being there when you're needed can sometimes be the most helpful gift of all.

- Let the teen know you want to be available when she needs someone to talk to, a shoulder to cry on, or just a companion. Tell her in advance that if she calls when you're not available to be sure and leave a message, and that you'll get back to her as soon as you can. Then honor your promise.

- Your presence, commitment, and concern can go a long way in helping someone through grief. You provide stability to someone who's life is presently in flux.

Carpe diem

Create an "I'm-Here-For-You" card that lets the teen know of your desire to be "on call" when she needs someone. Include your name, home phone number, work phone number, cell phone number and e-mail address, and the times and days when you're available. Deliver or mail the card to the teen.

78.

Give a candle.

- What do candles make you think of? Birthday parties? Romantic dinners? Church? Holidays? Other special occasions?

- Candles are soothing. There's a reason they're a significant part of many celebrations and rituals. When lit, they symbolize spirit, warmth, light, memories, love.

- You may want to let the teen's parents know you're giving him candles, particularly a younger teen, since candles can pose a fire hazard. Be sure the candle is dripless or comes with a fireproof container that will catch the melted wax.

Carpe diem

Give the teen a candle to light in memory of the person who died. Choose one that has special significance by virture of its shape, fragrance, or color. Attach a brief note and share your favorite memory of the person who died.

79.

Give a dream catcher.

- A peaceful night's sleep is one of the key ingredients for good mental, emotional, and physical health. Anxieties or nightmares, though, may keep a bereaved teen from getting the deep sleep she needs at a crucial time in her life.

- Giving the teen a Native American dream catcher may help soothe her mind so she can sleep with ease. The circle that frames a dream catcher represents the connection of all people in the world. The spider web design inside the circle is meant to capture the bad dreams of the universe's children.

Carpe diem

Buy or make a dream catcher for the teen. Suggest that she hang it above her bed or in a window in her room. Explain that the dream catcher is believed to catch bad dreams, and that the sun's morning rays will burn them away.

80.

Give a memory journal.

- One of the most helpful gifts you can present to a teen who's grieving is a memory journal with a handwritten set of instructions:

  - Use this book to record your favorite memories of the person who died. Use it to write down all the thoughts and feelings you experience after the death and as time goes on.

  - Paste in photos or magazine pictures, or copy down poems or lyrics that remind you of the person you've lost.

  - Yell at the world, rejoice in life—this is your private journal and is given with the hope it will comfort you and help you renew your zest for life.

  - Include photo corners and glue so the teen can paste in photos and other mementos.

- If you'd like, write an inscription at the beginning of the journal telling the teen how important he is to you and why.

Carpe diem

At a stationery store or bookstore, choose a journal or notebook that you think will appeal to the teen. Pick a nice pen to go with it. Give it to the teen with verbal or written instructions about its use.

81.

Give a memory box.

- A memory box is simply a special box that holds items that remind the teen of the person who died.

- The box can contain photos, letters, souvenirs, videotapes, linking objects and other items that help her remember the person who died.

- Ask others to contribute items to the memory box if the teen herself doesn't have photos or videotape footage.

Carpe diem

Give the teen a beautiful box of wood or paper-covered cardboard along with a note explaining its purpose. The box should be at least as big as a shoebox, preferably bigger, so all the teen's mementos will fit inside.

82.

Give a sleep basket.

- A teen who's grieving may have a difficult time falling asleep, especially during the first few months immediately following the death. This is normal and reflects her special needs right now. Still, there are many effective sleep-inducing techniques you can share that may help the teen.

- Reading in bed just before sleep is a relaxing ritual for many people. Give the teen a novel you think she'd enjoy—avoid thrillers, sci-fi, horror for this purpose—and suggest she read a chapter every night in bed.

Carpe diem

Fill a basket with items and ideas that will help the teen to sleep. Some things you might include: warm milk recipes, chamomile or Sleepy Time tea, a lavender sachet or scented candle, bath salts, a list of ideas for clearing the mind and relaxing the body.

83.

Stop by.

- E-mail, telephone, letters, texts—these are all good and convenient ways to support the grieving teen. But they don't replace good old-fashioned "face time."

- Did anyone ever stop by to visit you unexpectedly and end up making your day? Perhaps the visitor told a funny story, or wanted you to know she was just thinking of you. Maybe she brought you something or gave you a hug or invited you to an upcoming event.

- It's so easy to become isolated from the world these days that a personal visit can make you feel connected again to the human race.

Carpe diem

Visit the teen on a whim. Watch him at athletic practice
after school. Or stop by his house in the evening just
to say "hi." Keep your visit short and sweet.

84.

Turn feelings into something tangible.

- One thing that makes feelings hard to discuss is the fact that they're invisible. Yet identifying feelings and expressing them is a part of the human experience—and an important factor in healing and growth.

- With a little thought and creativity, you can describe feelings as something real. Anger could be a lion. Comfort might be lying on a soft cloud in a blue sky on a warm day. Loss, an empty paper bag blowing down a vacant street.

- Art is essentially thoughts and feelings made tangible. Take an art class with the teen. Set up canvases and paint.

Carpe diem

Help the teen identify and express her feelings by describing them as something tangible that exists outside of her body. Encourage her to share these descriptions verbally or write about them in a journal or in a letter to the person who died.

85.

Suggest safe ways for a teen boy to release his anger.

- Anger is a way for teens to say, "I protest this death" and vent their feelings of helplessness. Rage fantasies are also common. For example, if a teen's mom was killed in a car crash, the teen may express a desire to murder the driver at fault.

- Part of being a teen is toying with risky behavior and testing limits. When coupled with anger, these behaviors have the potential to be destructive.

- Driving recklessly, punching holes in walls, making violent threats, turning to alcohol, drugs, or promiscuity are some measures teenage boys may resort to when overwhelmed by anger.

- Exercise is a great way to release anger. Suggest a long run, raking leaves, hitting a punching bag, playing street hockey. Or get the teen involved in a sport.

Carpe diem

Blow up and tie off a bunch of balloons and have the teen write his angry thoughts on the balloons. When he has expressed everything that's been aggravating him, take the balloons to a basement, garage, or driveway. Tell the teen to stomp on the balloons until they've all burst—and then throw all that anger away.

86.

Suggest safe ways for a teen girl to release her anger.

- Anger is a way for teens to say, "I protest this death" and vent their feelings of helplessness. Rage fantasies are also common. For example, if a teen's mom was killed in a car crash, the teen may express a desire to murder the driver at fault.

- Part of being a teen is toying with risky behavior and testing limits. When coupled with anger, these behaviors have the potential to be destructive.

- Girls are often expected to better control themselves than boys—and that can make it difficult for girls to deal with a powerful emotion like anger. Girls get angry, too.

- Some teenage girls express anger through self abuse, reckless behavior, promiscuity and the abuse of alcohol and drugs.

- Since experiencing anger is part of life and part of grieving, it's important to offer teenage girls safe ways to vent their anger.

Carpe diem

Give the teen small pieces of paper on which she is to write everything she's angry about. Have her stuff each item inside a balloon, blow the balloon up, and then let it go. Molding clay, venting angry thoughts into a tape recording, and painting are other constructive ways of dealing with anger.

87.

Be on the look-out for "red flag" behaviors.

- To determine if the grieving teen needs extra help, it's important to distinguish between normal behaviors and dangerous ones:

Normal	Red Flags
Some limit-testing and rebellion	Fighting or legal troubles
Increased reliance on peers for support	Isolation from family and friends
Egocentrism	Chronic depression and low self-esteem
Increased moodiness	Dramatic change in personality or attitude
Increased sexual awareness	Inappropriate sexual behaviors
Impulsiveness/lack of common sense	Suicidal thoughts or actions
Eating disorders	Drug and alcohol abuse
Academic failure or overachievement	

- Because teens are going through a developmentally difficult time, we need to give them some leeway. Their frustrating actions are often normal. But "red flag" behaviors should be construed as a cry for help. Any behavior that indicates the teen might harm himself or others requires swift and decisive intervention.

Carpe diem

If the teen is being destructive, call another trusted adult right now and discuss your concern. Make a plan to intervene immediately. Involve the teen's parents if possible.

88.

Take a risk with the teen.

- For many teens, activities that harbor risk, real or perceived, are invigorating and life-affirming.

- Teens like to stretch limits the way it is. Grieving teens are especially attracted to risky activities.

- You can help by suggesting risk-taking activities that are safer than those the teen might dream up on his own. Some ideas: flying, bungee jumping, skydiving, rock climbing.

- Don't confuse appropriate risk-taking with self-destructiveness. The above activities require proper training, equipment and safeguards as well as parental permission.

Carpe diem

With his parent's permission, take the teen on a hot air balloon ride. Be sure to bring your camera to capture the moment.

89.

Take a walk together.

- Doing something outdoors with the teen is a great way to relieve stress and open up communication. The activity itself relieves the pressure of having to make conversation. Ironically, with this pressure removed, the teen may feel more at ease and more willing to talk about what's on his mind.

- Walking helps in other ways too. It moves the attention from the mind to the body and contributes to the teen's physical, emotional and spiritual health.

Carpe diem

Make a mental list of pleasant areas in the teen's community that are great places for walking. Make a date with the teen to go for a walk, just for the heck of it. Mention some places you think he'll enjoy, then let him choose—or offer to surprise him.

90.

Take care.

- In addition to caring about a bereaved teen's emotional needs, you can also be a positive influence where other needs are concerned. Is she eating at least three balanced meals a day? Dressing appropriately for the weather? Getting fresh air? Exercising? Interacting with others each day?

- A teen who's overwhelmed by grief may neglect even the simplest self-care activities, such as washing her face and brushing her teeth.

- Pick up the teen and take her out to get her hair cut, have a manicure, a pedicure or a facial.

Carpe diem

Assemble a "Take Care of Yourself" package for the teen with items like a toothbrush, soap, a washcloth, and some recipe cards with healthy snack ideas and exercise suggestions. Include a card reminding the teen to take care of herself each day.

91.

Donate a day to the teen.

- Time is such a rare commodity these days that when people give of their time, it truly is a gift.

- You may not know what to do or say to a teen who has recently lost someone she loved. But just being there can be a tremendous comfort.

- Respect the teen's wishes and mood. Don't force her to talk or do things she may not yet be up for.

- A day away from her everyday environment may be a refreshing change of pace. Drive to a nearby city and go shopping or drive to a state park and go for a hike.

Carpe diem

Offer to spend a day with the teen. You may be able to help with what she needs to get done that day, or perhaps you can best be of service by sitting quietly with her and listening.

92.

Focus on the day's happy moments.

- Every day contains at least one moment of happiness. It could be catching the sunrise at the height of its color and intensity, noticing a meadowlark's melody, exchanging a smile with a stranger, hearing an old song on the radio, enjoying a favorite food, laughing.

- It's easy to overlook these fleeting moments, but remembering them can decrease stress, lower blood pressure, and begin a chain reaction of happy thoughts.

- Make sure the teen understands that finding joy in each day does not mean she didn't love the person who died. Being sad and in mourning do not preclude happiness, especially as time passes.

Carpe diem

Make a point of talking to the teen today and asking her to share one happy moment from her day. Suggest that she write about that moment in her journal, or jot it on her calendar, and try to collect a week's worth of happy moments.

93.

Remember: One day at a time.

- Powerful emotions stemming from grief may lead the teen to believe he'll never be happy again. It's important to acknowledge those emotions and let the teen express how he feels.

- It's equally important to remind him that despite how he feels at this moment, he will continue to grow and live, and will again experience joy.

- Resuming his normal daily activities will help the teen to renew his commitment to life. "Losing himself" in his work allows him to direct his attention to the present moment.

Carpe diem

Help the teen re-establish a structure for his days. Have him make a checklist of what he needs to do and then prioritize it and check off each item when he completes it. Suggest that he try immersing himself in each activity, even if it's only for a few minutes.

94.

Be mindful of anniversaries.

- Anniversaries—of the death, life events, birthdays—can be especially difficult for mourners.

- Call the teen or spend the day with him and offer your support.

- Be direct; say, "I know your brother died a year ago today and I was thinking about you. What is this day like for you?"

- Planning an anniversary date activity in advance might be a welcome invitation for some teen mourners.

Carpe diem

Write down the anniversary of the death as well as the birthdays of the person who died and the teen in your daily planner. That way you won't forget the days that might be hardest for the teen.

95.

Don't be caught off guard by "griefbursts."

- Sometimes sudden, unexpected and strong waves of sadness will overtake the teen. These "griefbursts" can happen long after the event of the death.

- Griefbursts are normal but can be very scary and disheartening for the teen. "But I was doing so well and feeling so much better!" he might think to himself.

- Encourage the teen to talk to you or someone else when a griefburst bursts in. He doesn't need to cope with these intense feelings all alone.

Carpe diem

Package a small, special gift for the teen—perhaps a book, a CD or a candle—and tell him to tuck it away for a time when he's feeling especially sad. Include a supportive note.

96.

Leave the teen alone.

- A caution: If you were to follow all the guidelines in this book and to complete each and every recommended activity with the grieving teen, you would smother him! Sometimes the best way to help a grieving teen is to leave him alone.

- Grieving teens do need the love, support and ongoing presence of caring adults. But they also need down time. They need to hang out with other teens and they need time to be alone.

- Be sure to let the teen know that you'd like to spend some time with him when he's ready. If he rebuffs your invitations, don't be hurt. Instead, offer your support in less intrusive ways: write a letter, give a gift, send an e-mail.

- Intermittent and short-lived bouts of rebellion are normal. Grieving teens who withdraw for days and weeks at a time, however, may need intervention and extra help.

Carpe diem

The next time the teen rebels, keep your distance.
Send in another adult to try, instead.

97.

Educate others about the needs of grieving teens.

- When complicated by grief, a teen's developmental tasks can become more difficult. She may want to begin separating from her family, yet also feel a strong need for love and security. Simple daily tasks may suddenly seem complex.

- Instead of asking a teen to continue with school or work as if nothing happened, suggest a temporary shift in priorities that will allow her to experience her grief and gradually resume her normal responsibilities. Give her space, as well as love and support.

- Help the teen gradually resume her normal activities through planning. Offer coping mechanisms she can use when she's away from the security of home.

Carpe diem

Call several of the teen's most important teachers and explain what has happened. Ask for their support and understanding in the months to come.

98.

Follow up and follow through.

- This teen needs you right now. Follow up with him often in the weeks and months to come.

- Don't expect the teen to initiate contact. You call. You e-mail. You visit.

- If you've promised something (e.g. "I'll give you a call next week"), follow through. Now is definitely not the time to allow yourself excuses. Your unwavering and steadfast support teaches the teen that he is not alone and others are always there for him.

- Don't fade away in the months after the death. The teen may need you more six to eight months or even years after the death than he does right after the funeral.

Carpe diem

Phone the teen right this very minute—no procrastinating.
Don't think, "I'll do it tomorrow," because you may not.

99.

Understand that teens don't "get over" grief.

- As humans, we don't "get over" grief. The death of someone loved changes us irrevocably. We are never the same afterwards.

- Grieving teens don't "get over" grief, either. As they learn and grow, they adapt to it anew.

- But we can and do learn to "reconcile" our grief. That is, we learn to live with it and to incorporate what we have learned from it into our continued living.

- Each milestone in the teen's life (first boyfriend/girlfriend, prom, first job, high school graduation, etc.) may be bittersweet as he revisits his grief and reinterprets how the loss has affected his life.

Carpe diem

Keep in mind in all your interactions with the teen that he is changed forever by this death. Remember it is not your job to get him "over" grief but to help him mourn so he reconciles himself to it.

100.

Believe in the teen's capacity to heal.

- The most important quality you bring to the table in helping grieving teens is your belief in their capacity to reconcile the loss.

- Grieving teens are not "damaged goods." While they are irrevocably changed by the death, they are not "messed up for life" if they are given ample love and support throughout their grief journeys.

- If you truly believe that this teen can heal and go on to live a happy, full life, your optimism will color every moment you spend with her.

- Young people are resilient, strong, amazing creatures. With lots of love and support, they can not only integrate the loss, they can grow as a result of it.

Carpe diem

Be a witness to this teen's healing. As you see her making strides forward, congratulate her and honor her progress.

A Final Word

Thank you for being committed to "remembering" grieving teens. Too often teens become "forgotten mourners" because, in being so independent and separating themselves from adults, they don't seem to want or need our help. Wrong. Grieving teens *especially* need our love and support.

With this support, there is good reason to believe that grieving teens can integrate death into their lives and go on to live well and love well again. Many times I have been privileged to see young people not only heal, but grow through grief. They often emerge emotionally and spiritually stronger, more adaptable, more appreciative of life's joys.

I hope we meet one day and that you will share your experiences helping grieving teens with me. Until then, best wishes and Godspeed.

Send us your ideas for Healing A Teen's Grieving Heart!

I'd love to hear your ideas for helping grieving teens. I may use them in other books someday. Please jot down your idea and mail or e-mail it to:

Alan D. Wolfelt
The Center for Loss and Life Transition
3735 Broken Bow Road
Fort Collins, CO 80526
Or email me at DrWolfelt@centerforloss.com or go to our website, www.centerforloss.com.

I hope to hear from you!

My idea:

_____

_____

_____

_____

My name and mailing address:

_____

_____

_____

_____

ALSO BY ALAN WOLFELT

The Healing Your Grieving Heart Journal for Teens

With a Foreword by Brian Griese

Teenagers often don't want to talk to adults—or even to their friends—about their struggles. But given the opportunity, many will choose the more private option of writing. Many grieving teens find that journaling helps them sort through their confusing thoughts and feelings.

Yet few journals created just for teens exist and even fewer address the unique needs of the grieving teen. In the Introduction, this unique journal—written by Dr. Wolfelt and his 14-year-old daughter, Megan—affirms the grieving teen's thoughts and feelings and offers gentle, healing guidance. The six central needs of mourning are explained, as are common grief responses. Throughout, the authors provide simple, open-ended questions for the grieving teen to explore, such as:

• What do you miss most about the person who died?

• Write down one special memory.

• Which feelings have been most difficult for you since the death? Why?

• Is there something you wish you had said to the person who died but never did?

• Describe the personality of the person who died.

Designed just for grieving teens as a companion to Dr. Wolfelt's bestselling *Healing Your Grieving Heart for Teens: 100 Practical Ideas*, this journal will be a comforting, affirming and healing presence for teens in the weeks, months and years after the death of someone loved.

ISBN 978-1-879651-33-3 • 128 pages • softcover • $11.95

Companion

All Dr. Wolfelt's publications can be ordered by mail from:
Companion Press
3735 Broken Bow Road
Fort Collins, CO 80526
(970) 226-6050
www.centerforloss.com

ALSO BY ALAN WOLFELT

Sarah's Journey

Eight-year-old Sarah Johnson had always been her "daddy's little girl"—until the tragic day her father was killed in a car accident. Based on the belief that each child has the need to mourn in his or her own way, this book describes Sarah's grief experience and offers compassionate, practical advice for adults on topics such as regressive behaviors, explosive emotions, children and funerals, the grieving child at school and more.

ISBN 978-1-879651-03-6 • 121 pages • softcover • $9.95

Companion
PRESS

All Dr. Wolfelt's publications can be ordered by mail from:
Companion Press
3735 Broken Bow Road
Fort Collins, CO 80526
(970) 226-6050
www.centerforloss.com

ALSO BY ALAN WOLFELT

Healing Your Grieving Heart for Teens

100 Practical Ideas

In this compassionate book for grieving teenagers, Dr. Wolfelt speaks honestly and straightforwardly to teens, affirming their thoughts and feelings and giving them dozens of teen-friendly ideas for understanding and coping with their grief. The book also acknowledges teenagers' natural tendencies to spurn adult help while encouraging them to express their grief. Unlike longer, more text-dense books on grief, the one-idea-per-page format is inviting and readable for this age group.

ISBN 978-1-879651-23-4 • 128 pages • softcover • $11.95

Companion
PRESS

All Dr. Wolfelt's publications can be ordered by mail from:
Companion Press
3735 Broken Bow Road
Fort Collins, CO 80526
(970) 226-6050
www.centerforloss.com

ALSO BY ALAN WOLFELT

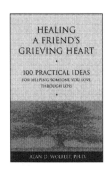

Healing A Friend's Grieving Heart

100 Practical Ideas for Helping Someone You Love Through Loss

When a friend suffers the loss of someone loved, you may not always know what to say. But you can *do* many helpful, loving things. Compassionate and eminently practical, *Healing A Friend's Grieving Heart* offers 100 practical ideas for friends, family members and caregivers who want to help. Some of the ideas teach the fundamentals of grief and mourning, while others offer practical, day-to-day ways to help. And each idea's carpe diem will help you seize the day by supporting your friend right now.

ISBN 978-1-879651-26-5 • 128 pages • softcover • $11.95

Companion
PRESS

All Dr. Wolfelt's publications can be ordered by mail from:
Companion Press
3735 Broken Bow Road
Fort Collins, CO 80526
(970) 226-6050
www.centerforloss.com

ALSO BY ALAN WOLFELT

The Journey Through Grief

Reflections On Healing
Second Edition

This popular hardcover book makes a wonderful gift
for those who grieve, helping them gently engage in
the work of mourning. Comforting and nurturing, *The
Journey Through Grief* doses mourners with the six needs
of mourning, helping them soothe themselves at the same
time it helps them heal.

Back by popular demand, we are now offering *The Journey Through Grief* again
in hardcover. The hardcover version of this beautiful book makes a wonderful,
healing gift for the newly bereaved.

This revised, second edition of *The Journey Through Grief* takes Dr. Wolfelt's
popular book of reflections and adds space for guided journaling, asking
readers thoughtful questions about their unique mourning needs and providing
room to write responses.

The Journey Through Grief is organized around the six needs that all mourners
must yield to—indeed embrace—if they are to go on to find continued meaning
in life and living. Following a short explanation of each mourning need is a
series of brief, spiritual passages that, when read slowly and reflectively, help
mourners work through their unique thoughts and feelings. *The Journey Through
Grief* is being used by many faith communities as part of their grief support
programs.

ISBN 978-1-879651-11-1 • hardcover • 176 pages • $21.95

Companion
P R E S S

All Dr. Wolfelt's publications can be ordered by mail from:
Companion Press
3735 Broken Bow Road
Fort Collins, CO 80526
(970) 226-6050
www.centerforloss.com